instant
interiors

instant interiors

quick fix ■ cheap chic ■ fast style

richard randall

David & Charles

A DAVID & CHARLES BOOK

First published in the UK in 2001

A catalogue record for this book is available from the British Library.

ISBN 0 7153 1096 8

Photography   **Simon Whitmore**

Commissioning editor   Lindsay Porter
Art editor   Ali Myer
Desk editor   Jennifer Proverbs
Designer   Rick Peel

Printed in Singapore by KHL
for David & Charles
Brunel House   Newton Abbot   Devon

contents

introduction

Home decorating is more popular than ever – the number of magazine articles and television programmes dedicated to the subject suggests it's our favourite pastime. In my work as a designer, I am constantly aware of new influences, and draw on these for inspiration for design ideas for the home.

When I began thinking about a book of home-decorating projects I wanted to address the needs of people who are just starting out, whether students, those in rented accommodation or first-time buyers. This presented some challenges, because it meant that the materials should be inexpensive – after all, who has a lot of money when they've just moved in to their own place? I also felt the ideas should be quick to do and easy to follow – most people already have enough going on in their lives without having to spend every spare minute decorating. Finally, I have noticed there is a real lack of good ideas that don't involve some sort of permanent make-over and, particularly if you are renting, you may not be in the position to paint the walls and strip back the floors, yet still want to make your mark on your immediate surroundings. For this reason, many of the ideas in this book are temporary – you can use them as a short-term solution, and even take them with you when you leave.

Organize excess clutter with these storage units custom-made from painted terracotta gas flues.

An overlooked window, such as one in a bathroom, can be frosted with glass-etching spray to create privacy without losing any natural light.

This book covers what I consider to be the key areas within the home – windows, wall and floors, lighting, storage and furniture. Whether you want to use all or just some of the ideas, if you address each of these areas in turn, you will be able to create a home environment that reflects your taste, rather than that of the previous occupant. I have included an additional chapter on concealment, especially intended for those who want to disguise wallpaper, cover a carpet that isn't to their taste, or who despair of ever organizing their clutter, and so need a way to hide it from view.

Each chapter includes a range of quick ideas and decorating projects that I hope you will find both easy and rewarding to make. Many of these require little or no DIY skills, such as customizing plain rugs and lampshades, using a ladder for storage, making beaded curtains and building a bench from lengths of timber. Other pieces however, require a little guidance and are accompanied by step-by-step instructions. To make life easier, I have listed all materials used and have paid particular attention to cost.

In my never-ending quest to keep expenses down, I have experimented with what may be considered unusual raw materials. Bricks, reclaimed timber, builders' pallets – these can all be used to create some great interior features and have the advantage of being easy to get hold of. Such materials also reflect today's trend for using industrial materials in all kinds of domestic settings.

I don't want to suggest that my ideas should be followed religiously. My aim is to encourage and, I hope, inspire. If you find my ideas are used as starting points for your own, so much the better! Every house should reflect the person living in it, so your interior should be an expression of your own thoughts and ideas, not mine. Ultimately, you will add your own personality to any of the decorating ideas you undertake. Because of this, I have tried to make the designs as adaptable as possible. Both the trellis screen and fixed bamboo blind

The trend for using industrial materials in a domestic setting inspired this taper holder.

described later in the book, for example, will have completely different characters depending on the fabric and colours you choose.

But how do you decide upon a design style? How do you know what your particular taste and design personality is? Flick through any magazine or turn on the TV and you will probably notice that today's interiors have become very much like the fashion industry. There are trends that come and go, seasonal colours, and ever-changing textures and patterns. With this amazing array of options it is not surprising that many of us just don't know where to start. Again, the advantage with many of the ideas in this book is that they will allow you to experiment to find your own taste and style – their simplicity means that you can enjoy creating something unique without feeling you have had to invest time and money to get it right.

When you want a change, simply start again! And if you find that one of the pieces of furniture or features you have devised or customized just gets better with age, then congratulate yourself on creating a design classic. Relax and enjoy it – it's your home, so have fun.

In planning and writing this book my aim was to inspire, stimulate and guide you to making your living environment as exciting and individual as the projects. Instead of relying on paint or colour to change a room, I wanted to show how to go one step further. By focusing on other aspects within the room you can easily add that all important finishing touch to your home. So why not have a go? Once you have started, there will be no stopping you!

Even if you don't attempt any of the projects, I hope that this book will inspire you to create the interior that works for you.

Good luck

Fabric stretched over wooden frames provides a quick cover-up for imperfect walls. Use wooden battens for the frame, then fix the fabric with staples.

Richard Randall.

walls and floors

quick fixes for walls and floors

Walls and floors are the starting point for decorating any room – with the right colours and textures you will set the scene for the rest of the decor, with the furniture, accessories and window treatments adding the elements of style. In some cases you may be lucky enough to start from scratch, with a blank canvas, or have the opportunity to change the existing decor. However, many of you will have to work with the existing decoration, aiming either to improve or disguise certain areas. Do not despair! There are many schemes that are easy to achieve, don't cost a fortune and will enable you to hide or draw attention away from features that are less than perfect.

Not all decorating solutions need be permanent and there are many ways to change your walls other than with paint or paper. Fabric is an excellent choice. Inexpensive fabrics will allow you to cover large surfaces in very little time and can be removed easily when you move house or want a change of scene. Look out for plain muslin, lining fabric or other lightweight material. Leave them plain or dye in the washing machine or by hand. Second-hand shops and markets are a good source for suitable fabrics, so allow yourself time to hunt around for unusual options. Think creatively: the answer may lie in a bedspread, bed linen, or several pieces of fabric sewn together.

If your floor will benefit from the addition of an inexpensive rug, consider creating your own, using acrylic paints on canvas, available from art supply stores. If you have the option to get rid of unsightly carpets, do so. Floorboards or concrete floors in good condition can be given an instant face-lift with a lick of paint.

Brightly coloured pom-poms can be used to add colour and interest to a plain rug.

creative flooring

For a quick floor make-over, look out for plain rugs and mats that can then be customized to suit your particular scheme. Decorate a basic rug in neutral colours with small multi-coloured pom-poms, available from craft shops and haberdashery departments. Fix them to the rug with glue or by hand-stitching, either in a random, all-over design or as a border. They add texture and a welcome splash of colour to an otherwise standard floor covering.

For a completely different look, create your own rug from artificial grass available from florist suppliers. Cut it into the shape of a lily pad and decorate with plastic flowers to make a durable, washable bath mat with real kitsch appeal.

If you are looking for something more permanent, but not too expensive, consider laying loft flooring panels. Made from chipboard, they can be painted to match you decor or left plain for an industrial look. For protection, seal with two or three coats of yacht varnish.

Apply yacht varnish for durability. Inexpensive loft tiles make an ideal floor-covering. Paint in the colour of your choice or leave plain for chic loft living.

disguising imperfections

Walls are not always in the best condition, but damp patches, small cracks or other marks can be covered with a range of temporary measures. I devised a solution involving fabric panels that can be hung over marks, and easily transferred when it's time to move on. To make each panel, you will need a wooden frame. This could be an artist's canvas, an old picture frame from a second-hand shop or one you make yourself from wooden battens. Stretch the fabric over the frame and attach at the back with staples, masking tape, fabric glue or nails. In addition to hiding small imperfections, you could use the panels to draw the eye away from a patterned wallpaper or place behind a bed as a dramatic backdrop.

Fake grass is both hard wearing and washable, and the ideal material for creating this fun, kitsch bathroom rug.

Laminated images are also a good way of covering small areas of wall. Most office-supply stores will laminate photographs, magazine cuttings or postcards. String them together using small metal rings, threaded through holes punched in the top and bottom of each image.

Another very simple but effective wall treatment can be created by hanging a length of lightweight fabric down the wall. I used second-hand sari fabric bought from a local market, but you could use coloured muslin, cheesecloth or any sheer fabric. Spray the fabric with a fire-retardant spray, available from department stores, then hang a string of lights behind the fabric for an extra romantic touch.

Giving walls and floors some thought and imagination allows you to solve initial problems, while creating solid foundations for a scheme for the rest of the room.

Personalize your walls with a series of laminated photographs attached with small metal rings. Use to hide small imperfections or to fill a blank space.

Sari fabric is easy to find in markets and comes in a range of stunning colours. Here, a length was suspended behind a bedhead, with a string of fairy lights behind for glamour.

connecting frames

Many people tend to go for the safe option when choosing a colour scheme for their home and some don't even have a say, especially if they are living in ready-furnished accommodation. So if you want to liven up plain walls, then this is the project for you.

Producing your own artwork will add instant individuality to walls. The idea behind this wall treatment is simple and inexpensive, yet extremely effective. It is made up of a grid of small frames, each containing a solid block of colour. Because the frames were so inexpensive, I was able to use a large number of them for real impact. To help select your colours use a paint chart, which you will find in any large DIY store. Once you have chosen a colour, copy the appropriate strip showing it in all its graduating tones. For a more personal approach, hang a series of photographs in the frames.

Whatever you choose, this grid of frames will add sophistication to any wall.

A grid of frames brings interest to plain walls. Frame solid blocks of colour in graduated shades for a contemporary look, or frame a collection of personal photographs.

how to...

materials and equipment

15 pine frames

white oil-based paint

2.5cm (1in) paintbrushes

sample pots of emulsion paint in five colours

pencil

ruler

metal hooks and eyes

Step 1

Remove the backing and any mount from the frames and set aside. Brush an even coat of white oil-based paint over the surface of each frame and leave to dry. Apply a second coat if required.

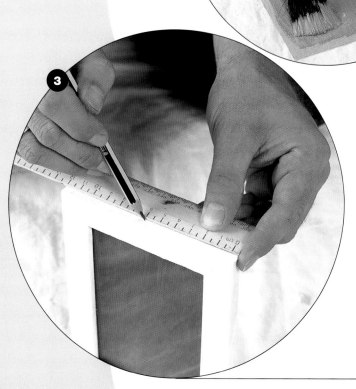

Step 3

Using a ruler and pencil, measure and mark the centre point along the top and bottom of each frame.

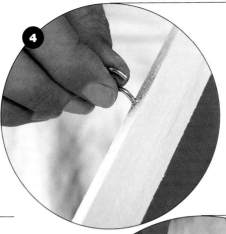

Step 4
Screw a hook into the top of 12 frames by hand (the remaining three will make up the top row) and an eye in the bottom of the remaining three frames plus nine others (the three with hooks but no eyes will make up the bottom row).

Step 2
Take the backing boards of each frame and paint three of them in the first emulsion colour, three in the second colour and so on until all 15 have been painted in the varying colours. Leave to dry.

Step 5
The frames are linked together in rows of five by hooking the eyes over the hooks.

Step 6
Working row by row, position those frames without hooks along the top and those without eyes along the bottom. Start with the lightest colour at the top, and graduate the colours downwards so that the darkest colour ends up at the bottom.

retro rug

When it comes to decorating and furnishing interiors, floors can often be neglected. By adding a rug you can introduce instant colour and pattern to a large area and establish the look of the room. Rugs can be very expensive, so for this design I've paid particular attention to cost and created a colourful rug that is both eye-catching and durable. It will enable you to make a strong statement and looks particularly good in a contemporary scheme, with minimalist, stream-lined furniture.

The rug is made from inexpensive door mats which come in a surprisingly good range of co-ordinating colours, and can be found in any department store. Each mat was cut in half, doubling the number of rectangles and colour combinations. It also has the added bonus of disguising the fact the rug is made from standard door mats. To create a retro look, round off the corners; square them off if you want the pieces to butt up neatly. The mats were then taped together to create a rug with real impact.

Inexpensive and extremely hard wearing, plain door mats can be taped together to create a stylish 1960s-style rug.

how to...

materials and equipment

six door mats

tape measure

chalk

metal ruler

craft knife

cutting mat or similar

card, for template

scissors

carpet tape

Step 1

Measure the two longer edges of each mat and mark the centre points. Chalk a line from point to point to divide each mat in half. Six mats were used here, giving 12 sections in all.

Step 2

Protect your work surface with a cutting mat or similar. Cut each mat in half by placing a metal ruler along a chalk line and cutting along it with a craft knife.

Step 3

The cut edges will no longer have curved corners, so you will need to cut these out. Take one half of the mat and place on top of the other half, so that the original curved corners lie on top of the cut edges. Draw around the curved outlines using chalk.

Step 4

To ensure a clean cut, and that all corners are the same size, cut a curved template from card. Position the card along a curved chalked line and use as a guide when cutting out each corner.

Step 5

Once you have cut out all the sections, experiment with different patterns and colour combinations. When you are happy with the design, turn each mat, face down, in position. Using carpet tape, secure by taping along all inner edges.

contemporary canvases

This idea developed as a direct response to the problem of damaged or cracked walls. The painted canvases not only work as a distraction, but on distressed walls the textured squares can make the background seem almost deliberate, creating the look of an urban loft apartment.

Each piece was created by stretching canvas over a wooden frame. I made my own frames by nailing four equal lengths of timber together, but inexpensive frames can be bought from art supply stores.

You could use professional artist's canvas, but heavy canvas from haberdashery departments tends to be a little cheaper and works just as well. As you will need a number of different coloured emulsion paints, the most economical option is to use sample pots. I roughly painted the canvases in a single colour, after applying a simple shape to the centre of each one, but you may wish to try painting stronger geometric designs or bands of colour. Keep it abstract for the best results.

Plain canvas stretched over simple wooden frames can be painted to create stunning textural works of art which will distract from the most unsightly walls.

how to. . .

materials and equipment

wooden battens

tape measure

pencil

jigsaw

hammer

nails

scissors

canvas

heavy-duty stapler

sample pots of
emulsion paint

2.5cm (1in)
paintbrushes

Step 1
To make a square frame
you will need to cut four
equal lengths of wood.
Decide on the size of the
finished frame, measure and
mark the required lengths
on a piece of wood and
then cut out using a jigsaw.

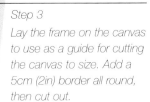

Step 2
Arrange the four lengths
of wood so that they make
a square, then secure by
nailing together firmly.

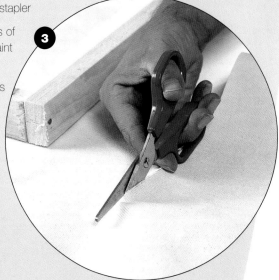

Step 3
Lay the frame on the canvas
to use as a guide for cutting
the canvas to size. Add a
5cm (2in) border all round,
then cut out.

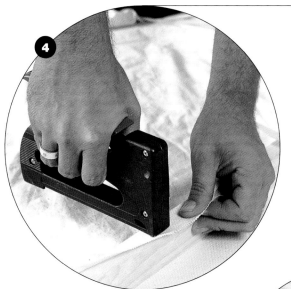

Step 4

Take one edge of the fabric and, holding it at its central point, pull it up and over the frame and staple in place. Repeat with the remaining three edges, securing the central point only. Staple the remainder of the fabric in place by working outward from each central point, while pulling the fabric taut.

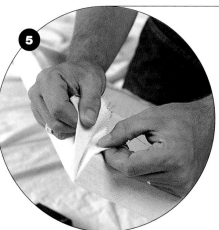

Step 5

For neat corners, fold in the excess fabric as you would the corners of a parcel, and staple tightly in place.

Step 6

Roughly paint a simple shape, such as a square or circle, in the centre of a canvas and leave to dry.

Step 7

Using the same colour, paint in the rest of the canvas, working outwards from the central shape. Keep the brushstrokes light, as the idea is to create a soft, subtle effect. You can always go over any areas that are too patchy.

windows

ways with windows

There are so many ways to dress windows, and so many different materials, effects and styles to choose from that you may not know where to begin. To start to narrow the field, first consider what you want from your treatment. Is it to be purely decorative? Does it need to block out light? Is it a means of creating privacy? Or do you require a combination of some or all of these? For example, there is little point in hanging thick curtains at a window that is constantly overlooked, as you will find they will be drawn for most of the time. This is fine if you don't mind the dark, but not a good idea if you want to make the most of available light. A better option in this case would be a combination of sheers and curtains, or a fabric or blind that allows light in while still retaining privacy.

Look at your window and assess how much light is being let in. Do you enjoy the view or would you rather block it out? There are plenty of ways to obscure an eyesore, such as your neighbour's bins, while still allowing light to filter into the room. Consider whether the window is draughty,

and if it would make sense to use heavy curtains as insulation – to close over a patio door in the evening, for instance.

Once you have established your requirements, you can start to consider the overall effect you want to create. Although there is a huge variety of ready-made curtains and blinds available on the high street, it is actually very easy to create imaginative, original window treatments yourself, often using unexpected materials. I've tried to achieve this in this chapter, and have looked at ways to customize windows, using economic means such as gluing, stapling, draping and even painting.

Beaded curtains are a great way to add accents of colour to a room, as well as having the obvious advantage of catching the light while partially obscuring a view outside. Add interest by combining chunky, round frosted and transparent glass beads with long wooden and metallic-finish beads.

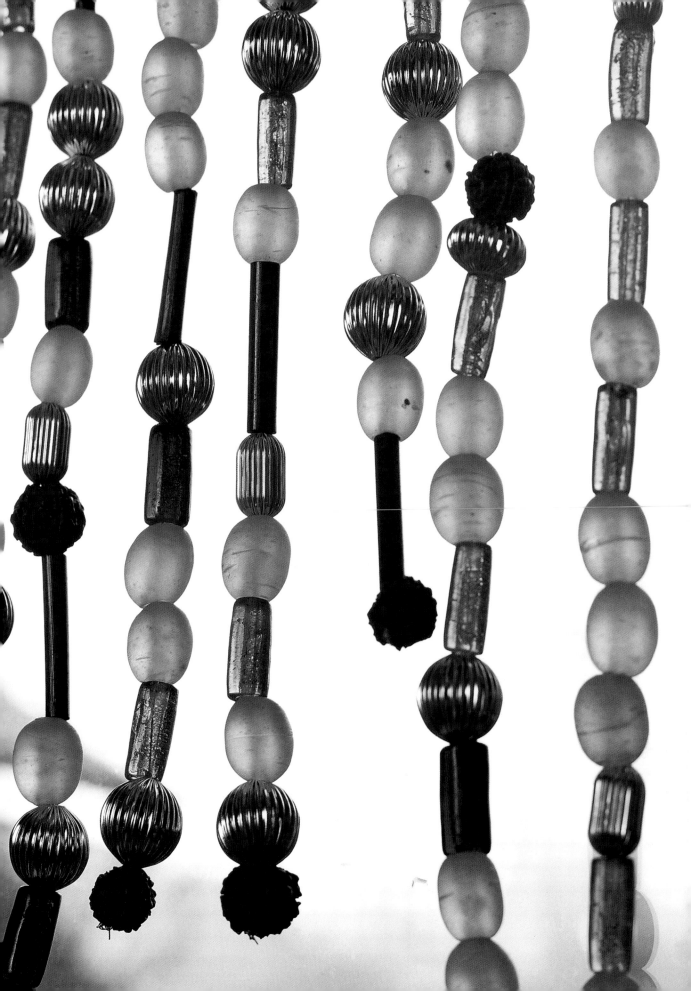

So now that you know what you want to achieve, there is still one important element to consider – the size of your window. Some treatments work best on a large scale. For example, generous lengths of fabric, whether inexpensive muslin or even a plain bedsheet, look great draped over a pole above a tall window, but would swamp smaller windows. In this instance you would be better off choosing a simple treatment such as a blind or panel of fabric.

creating privacy

Most homes contain at least one window that requires a degree of privacy without loss of light, so I've devised some simple screening devices. Taking stained glass as my inspiration, I used lens gels, available as ready-cut squares from specialist electrical shops, to liven up a kitchen door. I glued a different coloured square into each panel, creating a bold, bright look. You can buy the lens gels in sheets to cover larger areas of glass, or experiment by cutting them into smaller, mosaic-like pieces to create more complex patterns.

Glass-etching spray, available from art suppliers and DIY stores, provides another quick treatment. The spray is very easy to use – hold a little distance from your surface

Glass-etching spray creates a frosted effect on windows, and is a perfect way to create privacy without losing light. Before applying the spray, I cut different-sized circles from adhesive plastic and stuck them on the window. After the spray was dry, the circles were removed to reveal the pattern of clear glass underneath.

and apply in thin, even, coats then leave to dry. Use it to give opaque colour to the whole window, to frost individual panes or to create patterns. Cut shapes from adhesive-backed plastic and use to mask out areas you don't want to etch. When dry, remove the plastic shapes to reveal the pattern in clear glass. Another idea is to use a piece of old lace, held in place with masking tape. Apply etching spray, leave to dry, then remove to reveal the lace-effect on the glass.

Bead curtains provide a degree of privacy, allow in plenty of sun and are very easy to make. Thread your beads onto lengths of fishing wire. For a minimal effect, knot the wire between beads – as the light shines through, the wire will be barely visible, creating the effect of glistening beads hovering in mid-air. Mix different textures and materials and choose colours with an eye to the overall effect. If beads are too delicate for your room scheme, try fake flowers for a kitsch, fun look or a collection of colourful bottle tops – the choice is yours.

Inexpensive lens gels are used by photographers and lighting technicians to change the colours of their lights. Ready-cut squares were used to give this kitchen door a contemporary 'stained-glass' treatment. Use spray adhesive to stick the squares into each window pane. This technique couldn't be quicker and has the advantage of not being permanent: simply peel off the gel when you want a change.

minimalist blind

Roller blinds are among the simplest window treatments. Easy to install, their clean lines are perfect for smaller windows and as they are readily available in most department stores and very cheap, they really are the ideal no-fuss option. Roller blinds have the added advantage of being very easy to customize, so if you don't like what the shops have to offer you can create your own look.

This blind uses very simple decorating techniques combining painted stripes and cut-out squares to create a fresh, contemporary look. The stripes bring colour to the scheme, while the squares allow light to filter into the room. The resulting blind prevents the room from being overlooked, without having you go about your business in the dark. The whole blind was finished off with a length of decorative beading.

A plain roller blind is basically a blank canvas that can be painted, stencilled, splattered or transformed in any way you like.

how to...

materials and equipment

plain canvas roller blind

pencil

masking tape

spray paint in two colours

metal ruler

craft knife

cutting mat or similar

decorative wooden beading

hacksaw

strong all-purpose glue

Step 1

To plan the position of the stripes, open out the blind to its full length and mark the stripes with a pencil. Use masking tape to cover the areas of the blind that should be left unpainted or painted in the second colour. Working in a well-ventilated area, spray the first colour and leave to dry.

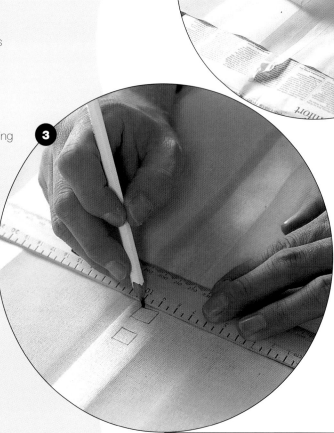

Step 3

Using a pencil and ruler, draw small squares within the striped areas. In this design they were grouped in twos and threes as the slightly random, asymmetrical composition of the squares adds to the modern feel of the finished design.

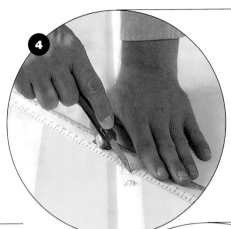

Step 4

Working on a cutting mat or similar, cut out the squares using a craft knife and a metal ruler. First cut crosses, corner to corner, in the squares, then cut around the outside edges.

Step 2

When completely dry, remove the masking tape. Repeat the masking process, this time covering all the previously painted areas with tape, plus any remaining areas to be left plain. Spray with the second colour and leave to dry. Remove the masking tape as before.

Step 5

Measure the length of beading required for the bottom edge of the blind, and cut to fit. In a well-ventilated area, spray the beading in one of your chosen colours and leave to dry.

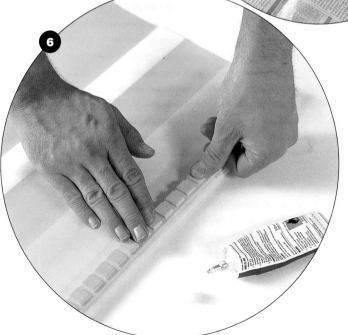

Step 6

Glue the beading along the bottom edge of the blind. Once dry, hang the finished blind following the manufacturer's instructions, using the fixings supplied.

draped sheers

Lace, net and voile are common materials for dressing windows, as not only do they screen you from outside eyes but still allow light to enter the room. This window treatment evolved from that idea, and demonstrates how you can achieve the same amount of privacy as with a traditional net curtain but with a more up-to-date look. So if you want to be shielded from the outside world, particularly in a front-facing room, this idea is definitely for you.

I started with a generous amount of dressmaker's chiffon. It is very sheer, comes in a huge range of colours, and is surprisingly inexpensive so you don't have to skimp on the amount used. I then embellished the material with silk flowers bought from a local market. Finally, the fabric was looped over curtain wire with the top layer pulled back from the window. A layer of chiffon was left hanging, allowing light in, while infusing the window with vibrant colour.

This curtain used a length of fabric twice as long as the window. Using longer lengths will not only create truly dramatic drapes but will allow the chiffon to lie in pools of colour on the floor.

how to...

materials and equipment

dressmaker's chiffon, slightly wider than your window, and at least twice its length

needle and matching thread

small silk flowers on stalks

scissors

fabric glue

cup hooks

curtain wire with eyes

tassel tieback

wall hook, for tie-back

Step 1

Sew a small hem along the top and bottom edges of your fabric. Remove the flowers and leaves from their stalks and, using fabric glue, stick the flower heads along both side edges of the chiffon. Depending on the width of your fabric you may not need to hem the edges, because of the selvage.

Step 2

Glue a random scattering of leaves over the fabric. I aimed for a fairly even spacing of leaves, which can be judged by eye as it doesn't need to be exact.

Step 3

Glue a single flower head in the centre of each leaf, alternating the colours as you go.

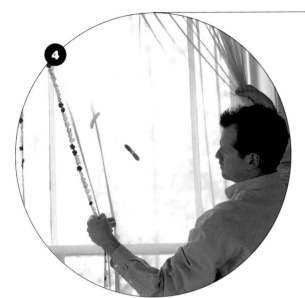

Step 4

Screw a cup hook into each top corner of the window frame, by hand, and use to suspend a taut length of curtain wire. Hang the fabric over the wire, so that you have two equal lengths of fabric at the window. Allow the bottom length to cover the whole window.

Step 5

Gather the top piece of fabric and pull to one side of the window. Hold in place with a tassel secured with a hook screwed into the window frame. Allow the top fabric to fall in a generous drape.

bamboo blind

One of the strengths of this window treatment is its flexibility. The basic blind is incredibly easy to make but, depending on the materials you use, you can alter the entire look of the finished piece. All you need to remember is that, as the blind cannot be raised, you must use a sheer or open-weave fabric in order to let light through.

I've chosen to use natural materials – bamboo, raffia, and webbing – to create an 'organic'-looking blind. Surround the window with plants and team with neutral, heavily textured fabrics such as hessian, canvas and muslin to create a safari look. For a completely different feel, try painting the bamboo framework with pale-coloured emulsion and pairing with a floral chiffon fabric. The effect will be light, airy and romantic. If that's not for you, use chrome poles instead of bamboo and team with silver fabric, for a window with a contemporary edge.

This versatile fixed blind can be adapted to suit any decor – all you need is a basic frame with a complementary sheer fabric and you'll never need to consider using net curtains again.

how to...

materials and equipment

tape measure

pencil

bamboo poles

hacksaw

natural string

scissors

natural raffia

mesh fabric, large enough
to cover the bamboo frame

strong all-purpose glue

masking tape (optional)

cup hooks

Step 1

*The blind should fit over the
entire window frame.
For the length, measure
from the top of the frame to
the window sill or below. For
the width, measure from the
outside edge of the frame to
the other. Add 10cm (4in) to
each of the measurements,
then cut two poles for the
width and two for the length.*

Step 3

*The raffia is used as
decoration, however, it will
help strengthen the corners
of your blind. Wrap it over
the string, ensuring it covers
the string completely, then
knot to secure, as before.*

Step 4

Measure the size of the completed frame and cut a piece of fabric to this size. I found the easiest way to do this was to lay the frame directly on the fabric, mark the dimensions with a pencil then cut the fabric to size.

Step 2

Lay out the bamboo poles to create a frame, overlapping them at each corner by 2.5cm (1in). Tightly bind the first corner with string, tying off in a knot to secure. Check the corner is at right angles before moving onto the next, and so on, until you have the completed frame.

Step 5

Working on the right side of the fabric, apply glue around all edges. Press firmly in place to the back of the frame. (Use a little masking tape to hold the fabric in place while the glue dries.)

Step 6

Screw a cup hook by hand into each top corner of the window frame. Hang the blind by resting the bamboo frame on the hooks.

concealment

clever cover-ups

An entire chapter devoted to concealment may seem excessive but I feel it is an absolute must. No matter what type of accommodation we live in there are always items or areas of the house that are better hidden from sight. Whether it as simple as a hi-fi system or a heap of washing on the floor, or something more permanent such as a damp patch on a wall or ugly pipework, there is always room for improvement.

Of course there are many products on the market you can buy, such as customized units for hi-fi and television sets, computer work-stations and numerous screening devices, but these tend to be expensive. Although I know few people who would not benefit from buying those inexpensive cable collectors to tame the mass of wires that seems to invade every home, for the most part, I believe it is more fun and rewarding to come up with your own solutions.

Think about your decor and what will work within your home. Lengths of fabric hung in front of a washing machine or open kitchen units will enhance a country-style kitchen, while all manner of inexpensive roller or bamboo blinds can be fitted at the top of untidy alcoves or shelves and drawn down to the floor. If you want to hide the trappings of modern-day living completely, try adapting a second-hand hand cupboard to hide a TV – just cut a hole in the back to take the wires. Look through magazines and catalogues for inspiration and once you begin to explore the possibilities you'll be amazed at how easily the ideas flow.

Detract from bathroom tiling with layers of bubble wrap or plastic-backed fabric hung from an ordinary shower pole. These materials are ideal for use in the bathroom as they are water resistant.

screening and disguising

One simple answer to all your problems is a
screen, and one of the ideas developed later
in this chapter includes a screen made from
garden trellis that can be adapted to suit
your scheme. However, for a more
contemporary look you may want to consider
a screen made from a sheet of opaque
greenhouse insulator (see opposite page).
Inexpensive sheeting in various sizes is
available from your local garden centre. The
sheet used here measures 180 x 90cm
(6 x 3ft) but the size can be adapted as
necessary. Score a vertical line down the
sheet every 30cm (12in), using a craft knife
and metal ruler, then fold the sheet
concertina-style along each line to create
what appear to be individual panels. The
resulting piece of contemporary design is
ideal for screening objects such as a hi-fi,
video and tv system.

If there is something larger and more
permanent that you wish to conceal, then
once again a screen is an option. But in
smaller areas where this would prove a
hindrance why not try using bubble wrap,
available from stationery and office supply
shops. Just hang as you would a shower
curtain – as it is inexpensive, you can be
generous with the amount you use and,

These can be glued or fixed in place with panel pins. Boxing in pipework is not always an option. Here, decorative mdf strips were used as a disguise.

what's more, it is totally waterproof. Use to hide old tiling or a battered shower – the unusual treatment will take your mind off the fact the bathroom suite is not as innovative as the wrap.

For many of us, pipes are a major eyesore, especially in the kitchen, as the eye tends to be attracted to them immediately. Try running scalloped mdf strips along the pipes to conceal them. Ready-cut mdf strips are available in different shapes, but wooden mouldings or planks of timber shaped using a jigsaw would work equally well. You'll find your ugly pipes are transformed into a major feature of the room.

A screen can be used to disguise or conceal almost anything. Greenhouse insulator sheeting is not only inexpensive but extremely flexible and can be scored and bent into simple panels. Because it is so portable, one day it may be used to hide an unsightly wall or a pile of clothes, while another it may become a neat way of screening off a work area.

radiator cover

Radiators rarely add much in the way of visual style to a room, and most of us would agree that they would benefit from being disguised in some way. Painting them the same colour as the wall will help them blend in, but the ideal solution would be to cover them. If you choose this option make sure the cover does not block the flow of heat into the room.

Made-to-measure covers are now readily available but can be expensive, so I've devised this simple cover using a ready-made shelf and fretwork panel, available from DIY stores. It's cheap, easy to assemble, and allows the maximum amount of heat into the room. When hanging any shelf above a radiator leave a gap at the back of the shelf to allow heat to circulate.

This simple cover uses a ready-cut fretwork panel to disguise the radiator. The fretwork allows air to circulate and is available in a range of shapes.

how to...

Step 1

Apply an even coat of oil-based paint to the entire surface of the shelf and shelf brackets. Leave to dry. Apply a second coat and leave to dry.

materials and equipment

ready-made shelf and wooden brackets, slightly longer than the radiator

oil-based paint

5cm (2in) paintbrush

mdf fretwork, 6mm (¼in) thick and large enough to cover the front of the radiator

hammer

nails

screwdriver

screws

tape measure

timber batten (see step 3 for required length)

hacksaw

drill

masonry bit

wall plugs

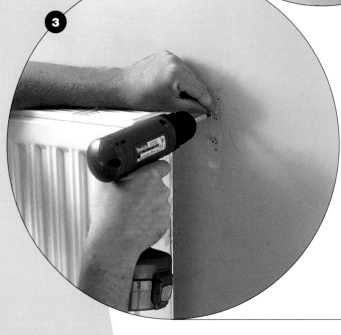

Step 3

Place the brackets in position on the underside of the shelf, making sure they protrude by 2.5cm (1in) at the back. Nail or screw to the shelf. Measure the distance between the brackets and cut a length of timber to this length. Position on the underside of the shelf, in between the brackets, and approximately 1.2cm (½in) back from the front edge. Nail in place as before.

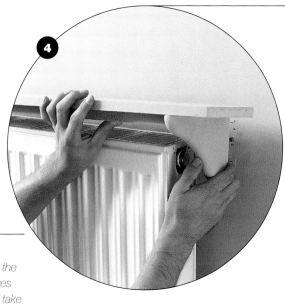

Step 4

Hold the shelf in place against the wall and mark the position of the bracket fixings. Drill and plug the holes. Fix screws into the holes – do not screw them flush with the wall, but stop short, so that the neck of each screw protrudes from the wall. Hang the shelf on the screws.

The inbuilt fitting of the bracket allows it to be fixed easily to the wall.

Step 2

Paint the fretwork using the same paint as the shelves and brackets. This may take longer than you think, as painting the inner area of the cut-out sections can be time consuming. Once dry, repeat with a second coat.

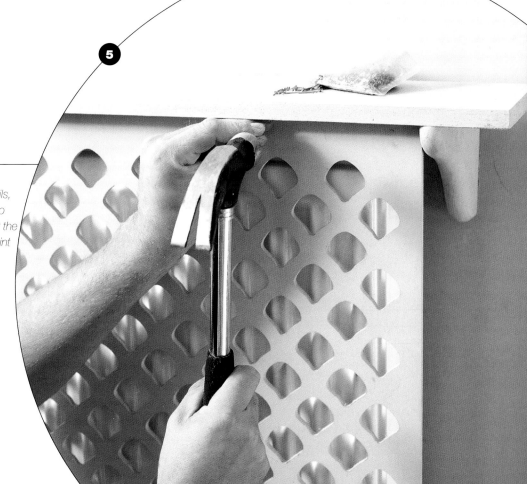

Step 5

Using a hammer and nails, tack the fretwork panel to the timber batten. Cover the nail heads with a little paint and leave to dry.

trellis screen

A screen provides the perfect cover-up and can be moved wherever needed or folded away when not in use. It can be created in such a range of styles, from theatrical glamour to minimalist chic, that it can become a stunning feature in its own right.

I've used garden trellis for this project as it is inexpensive and available from DIY stores across the country. The trellis was painted black with a high-gloss finish to create a Japanese, lacquered look. However, you can easily adapt the style to co-ordinate with your own interior. Choose a different paint colour and back the trellis with an alternative material such as wrapping paper or fabric to create a totally different feel – why not try a soft voile in the bedroom or vibrant plastic-coated fabrics in the kitchen ?

Wherever and however you use this screen you'll soon see just how useful it is.

This decorative Japanese-style screen works particularly well in today's modern interiors. Use it to hide clutter or to divide a room into separate areas.

how to...

materials and equipment

four garden trellis panels

medium-grade sandpaper

fine-grade sandpaper

black emulsion paint

4cm (1½in) paintbrushes

clear gloss varnish

greaseproof paper

tape measure

pencil

scissors

heavy-duty stapler

cable ties

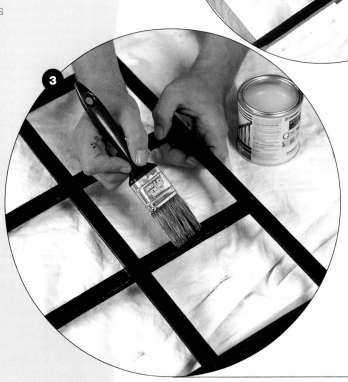

Step 1

As exterior trellis is made from fairly rough cuts of wood, you will need to sand it before painting. Start with medium-grade paper to remove any large imperfections then finish with fine-grade paper to ensure a smooth surface.

Step 3

Seal the painted panels with one or two coats of clear varnish. Leave to dry.

Step 4

Lay the trellis panels on top of a sheet of greaseproof paper. With the aid of a tape measure, draw around each section of trellis and cut out.

Step 2

Paint all four trellis panels with black emulsion and leave to dry. You may find that you need to apply a second coat in order to achieve even coverage.

Step 5

Place a greaseproof paper panel on the back of each trellis panel and staple in place along all wooden sections.

Step 6

To join the panels together, place side by side on a flat surface, making sure all top and bottom edges are level. Working at regular intervals down each pair of adjoining sides, thread cable ties through one panel and out through the other, and secure in place.

fabric panel
with pockets

This simple no-sew project is ideal for large areas, as it is functional, decorative and inexpensive. The pockets provide storage for all those bits of clutter that accumulate and are also a great way of displaying treasured collections or even photographs.

This panel was specifically designed to hang in an alcove, where it instantly disguises overflowing shelves. It is equally effective hanging directly on a wall to cover up unsightly wallpaper or damaged patches. If made from waterproof fabric, the panel could be used to conceal worn tiling in the kitchen or bathroom, while a smaller panel could be made to hang in the hallway to store shoes.

Any of these variations will allow you to hide imperfections while providing extra storage space, demonstrating just how versatile this idea is.

This fabric panel was made to fit in an alcove and could be used to hide unsightly wallpaper, ugly pipework or clutter. The decorative pockets provide additional storage for small items.

how to...

materials and equipment

fabric, such as muslin, cotton or canvas

tape measure

scissors

iron-on fabric tape

iron

fabric glue

pencil

small cup hooks

drill

masonry bit

wall plugs

curtain wire with eyes

Step 1

Measure the width and height of the area for the panel, adding a 5cm (2in) seam allowance on all sides. Cut the fabric to size. Place iron-on fabric tape along all four sides, fold over a 5cm (2in) hem all round and iron in place.

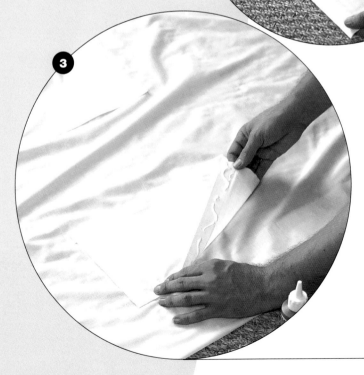

Step 3

Measure and mark the position of each pocket on the main fabric panel. Apply fabric glue to three sides of each pocket, leaving one short edge free. Stick the pockets to the panel, ensuring the free edge faces upwards to create the pocket opening.

Step 4

Measure and mark the position of the hooks on the wall from which the wire will hang. Drill and plug the holes, before screwing the hooks in place by hand. Thread the wire through the top hem of the panel, ready for hanging.

Step 2

Decide on the number and size of pockets you want – I used 12 pockets each measuring 10 x 12.5cm (4 x 5in) – add a 2.5cm (1in) seam allowance on all sides and cut out. Turn in a 2.5cm (1in) hem all round and fix in place with iron-on tape as for the main panel.

Step 5

Loop the curtain eyes onto the hooks, then distribute the panel fabric evenly along the curtain wire.

Step 6

Fill the pockets with display items such as postcards, letters, dried flowers or leaves, or use as storage for shoes, accessories or other small-scale items.

storage

stylish storage solutions

Storage problems can be so diverse, that when I was compiling this chapter my aim was to create flexible solutions that can be adapted to suit your own demands.

Before you splash out on any new storage systems, it is a good idea to take a long hard look at your present storage and organize it. Throw away anything you don't really need. Once you stop hoarding you'll be surprised at how much space you can create. Then, look at the things you need to store and ask yourself the following questions: Do you want them hidden from sight or on display? Can you adapt your existing storage systems or do you need to create more? Make a note of what catches your eye when you walk into a room. Is there always an untidy pile of videos on show, a corner full of toys or a stack of clothes? Assess each room accordingly.

Now that you know what you need to store, think about the space you have and what you want from it. Are there any obvious areas, such as empty walls or nooks and crannies that can be utilized? Could you build high cupboards for those items that are not in everyday use? A trip to your local high street, and a flick through some mail order catalogues, will not only result in your finding great products, but might also inspire one or two ideas that you can put into practice yourself. Look out for cheap and cheerful containers such as large baskets which can be stacked, boxes that can be covered to match your decor, or bags that can be hung on the wall. A curtain pole screwed to the wall is ideal for hanging pots and pans, while a clothes bin can be

A simple wooden ladder, which can be bought or made from lengths of timber, makes an effective display and storage unit. Paint to match the decor, then screw cup hooks into the steps to hang small items.

used to store toys. In fact, with a little imagination, most of us can create our own storage solutions for a fraction of the cost of ready-made items.

Modern storage tends to be very open plan so rather than hiding your treasured possessions away in a cupboard you can now store them while still keeping them on display. This makes for obtainable solutions that are decorative as well as functional and, as I hope this chapter proves, very easy to achieve.

simple storage

My solutions for storage may be simple, but they are highly effective. A ladder, for instance, standing against a wall is a great aid to any room as you can easily hang all sorts of items from it. I've sprayed a ladder red so that it becomes a decorative piece in its own right. By screwing a few hooks into some of the steps, it is instantly transformed into a stylish kitchen unit for hanging utensils or tea towels. In the bathroom it can be used as a modern towel rail or stand it in a bedroom to show off your favourite accessories.

Most of us at some time in our lives will require a little more organization at home. Maybe it doubles up as your place of work, or you need more space for clothes or a

When planning extra storage, walls are often forgotten. Utilize these by screwing ready-made wooden boxes to the wall. Paint them in contrasting colours, then hang randomly for an abstract display.

video or CD collection that is ever-expanding. A solution can be found in the versatile wooden boxes that can be bought at most DIY or department stores. Paint in a range of colours, then hang them on the wall to create an attractive and useful display that can be added to as and when required. For smaller items, add a shelf or two so that the objects can be neatly pigeon-holed.

I like to use unusual materials whenever possible, and a brickyard is the perfect place to visit when looking for storage solutions. Inexpensive terracotta gas flues were bought at a local yard and painted in contrasting colours. Stacked on the floor they make a casual yet effective storage unit for CDs. For a more formal arrangement, they could be mounted on the wall.

Storage in general has become more relaxed in recent years, as our interiors become an extension of our personalities. So whenever possible combine storage with decorating and display, and let people see what interests you by showing them what you collect.

Bold colours and simple shapes lend themselves perfectly to high impact, yet practical, storage as demonstrated by these painted and stacked terracotta gas flues.

customized shelving

The most basic form of storage in any room is shelving. In a bathroom where the only available space is often the walls, shelves are the obvious answer, as they avoid cluttering up limited surface areas around baths and sinks.

For this project I adapted a ready-made shelf, available from all DIY stores, to create an alternative type of storage that caters for the many items that need organizing in the bathroom. Cut out circles from the shelf, then sink a plastic beaker into each hole. These are not only useful for storing objects that aren't so pleasing to the eye, but are ideal for smaller items that may get lost, such as brushes, cotton wool and so on. Hooks screwed underneath the shelf provide an extra dimension as they can be used to keep towels or face clothes clean, dry and easily within reach.

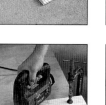

Transform ready-made shelving by adding storage beakers and hooks. The result is great in a bathroom for storing toiletries or in a study for keeping desk-top clutter neat and tidy.

how to...

materials and equipment

ready-made shelf and wooden brackets

tape measure

pencil

plastic beakers

clamp

drill

large wood bit

jigsaw

medium-grade sandpaper

oil-based paint

5cm (2in) paintbrush

cup hooks

masonry bit

wall plugs

screws

screwdriver

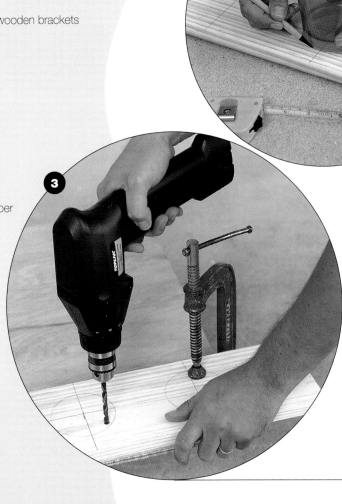

Step 1

Measure the length of the shelf and divide into four equal sections to give you three marked points.

Step 3

Clamp the shelf to the work surface. Fit the drill with the wood bit and drill a hole on the inside edge of a circle, large enough to take the jigsaw blade.

Step 4

Insert the jigsaw blade into one of the pre-cut holes and, following the pencil lines, cut out the first circle.

Step 2

Place one of the beakers on a marked point, centring it on the line and between the front and back edges of the shelf. Draw around the beaker base. Repeat at the other two marked points to create three circles.

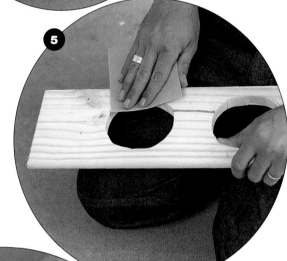

Step 5

Drill and cut out the remaining two circles, then sand all the sawn edges smooth.

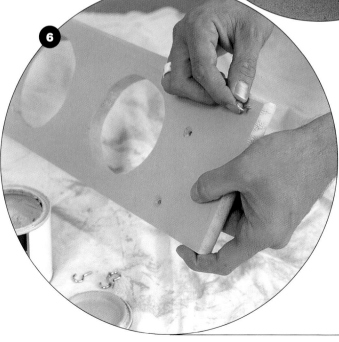

Step 6

Apply two coats of paint to the shelf and brackets. Once dry, screw cup hooks to the underside of the shelf, by hand. (I attached a hook at one end only.) Attach the brackets to the shelf using the fixings provided. Hold the shelf against the wall and mark the position of the bracket fixings. Drill and plug the holes. Fix the screws into the holes and hang the shelf. Place the beakers in position.

folding
shelf-unit

This piece was created especially for those who never seem to have enough storage space. An ordinary wooden clothes airer was adapted to create a versatile storage unit that can be used throughout the house. The detachable shelves allow you to assemble it whenever and wherever you want, and it can be folded away and stored when no longer required. What's more, it doesn't cost a fortune to make.

The clothes airer was treated with a metallic spray paint, which is quick and easy to apply and gives the wood a subtle sheen. The shelves were made of mdf covered with wadding and quilted fabric, providing an interesting contrast with the metallic effect of the frame. If you feel this particular scheme is too monochromatic, choose a matt emulsion paint and a softer fabric to match your interior.

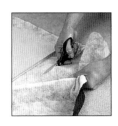

A wooden clothes airer can be turned into a useful storage unit by the addition of fabric-covered mdf shelves. Use around the home to store clothes, linen, towels or pots and pans.

how to...

materials and equipment

wooden clothes airer

tape measure

pencil

mdf, 6mm (¼in) thick

jigsaw

strong all-purpose glue

wadding (see step 3 for quantities)

scissors

quilted fabric (see steps 4 and 6 for quantities)

heavy-duty stapler

all-purpose silver spray paint

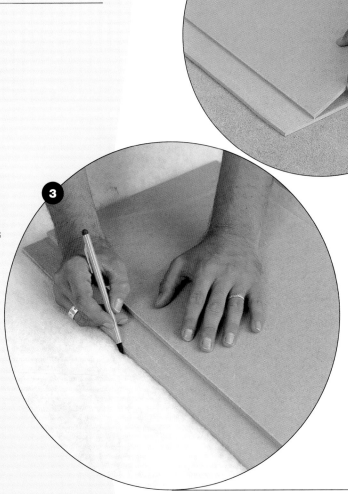

Step 1
Stand the airer upright and measure the width of the rails, and the depth between the front and back rails. Add 10cm (4in) to the depth measurement, then cut the mdf shelves to this size.

Step 3
Place each mdf shelf on top of the wadding. Draw around the larger outline with a pencil and cut out.

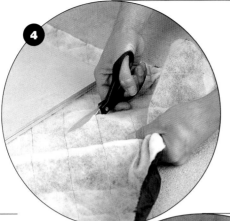

Step 4

Lay the fabric face down on a flat surface and place the wadding on top. With the larger section of the shelf facing downwards, position on top of the wadding. Using the shelf as a guide, cut out the fabric, leaving a 10cm (4in) border all round.

Step 2

Working from the inner edge of each rail, measure the depth between the back and front rails. Using the same width measurement as before, cut pieces of mdf to this size – you will need one per shelf. Glue a small section of mdf to the centre of each large shelf piece and leave to dry.

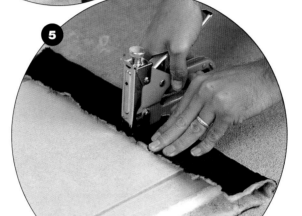

Step 5

Turn over all four edges of the fabric and staple to the back of the mdf shelf, pulling the fabric taut as you go. Snip diagonally across the excess fabric at each corner, fold neatly onto the back of the mdf and staple in place.

Step 6

Cut a piece of fabric large enough to fit the back of the shelf. Turn in the raw edges and glue to the back of the shelf to hide the raw, stapled edges. Cover the remaining shelves in the same way. Working in a well-ventilated area, spray the airer with paint, applying in thin coats to build up the colour. Once dry, slot the shelves in position.

cd holder

Car boot sales, second-hand stores and charity shops are great places for finding pieces of furniture that can be turned into inexpensive storage – all they need is a little attention. This filing cabinet, ideal for storing CDs, was found at a car boot sale. The decorative treatment it received can be used to give any bargain-buy a make-over.

A decoupage technique using bright, cheerful images was the perfect solution for renovating the surface. I used a Polaroid camera to take pictures that were then photocopied and enlarged at a local office supply store – this is inexpensive so you can photocopy more than you think you'll need, to allow for error. If you don't have a Polaroid camera, flick through photo albums and pick out your favourite snap shots, or cut images from magazines or wrapping paper. It is then simply a case of sticking the images to the unit. For a modern touch and greater mobility add wheels to the base of the cabinet.

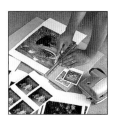

Create a unique storage unit by covering a second-hand filing cabinet with photocopied images, glued in place. Use to store CDs or computer disks.

how to...

materials and equipment

small wooden or metal filing cabinet

medium-grade sandpaper

wood or metal primer

5cm (2in) paintbrushes

selection of images (such as photographs or magazine cut-outs)

metal ruler

craft knife

cutting mat or similar

masking tape

spray adhesive

artist's paintbrush

silver paint

clear water-based varnish

4 castors

screwdriver

screws

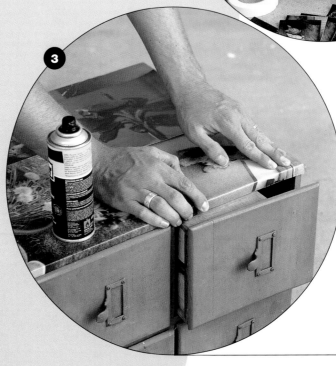

Step 1
Prepare the surface of the cabinet by sanding lightly. Apply a coat of primer and leave to dry. Using a photocopier, enlarge the selected images at various sizes. You will need enough copies to cover the entire surface of the unit. Trim away any white edges left on the copies.

Step 3
Working in a well-ventilated area, spray the back of each picture with glue, then press into position. Make sure that all the edges are well stuck down and the images lie flat without any wrinkles or air bubbles.

Step 4
To seal the images and create a wipe-clean surface, apply one or two coats of clear varnish over the entire surface of the box.

Step 2
Before gluing the pictures in position, experiment with different designs and layouts. Hold the images in place temporarily with masking tape.

Step 5
Using an artist's paintbrush, apply a coat of silver paint to the handles and leave to dry.

Step 6
Screw the castors in position at each corner on the underside of the finished storage box.

furniture

fast furniture

If you are looking for a quick way to improve your interior, you may be surprised to hear that a change of furniture could be the answer. Sometimes all you need to determine a style instantly is one key piece – and it needn't break the bank. In this chapter I aim to address several types of furniture, both in style and function, and to demonstrate just how effective a well-chosen piece can be in establishing a look.

As with any form of decoration, ask yourself several questions before either buying or making a piece of furniture. Are you hoping that it will detract from its surroundings, or do you want to emphasize a particular look? Does it need to harmonize with other elements in the room or are you going for a bold statement to create a focal point? Remember to consider the function of the piece to determine what materials it should be made from.

In this chapter I was particularly interested in transforming basic, inexpensive materials, such as breeze blocks, pasting tables and wire baskets into original pieces of furniture, with the minimum of practical skills. All the ideas were designed with the following considerations in mind: practicality, design, durability and, of course, cost.

Turn a railway sleeper and wooden plank into a bench that can be used inside and out. A cushion in a luxurious fabric softens the industrial feel of the hard-wearing wood.

constructing simple designs

Although the pieces in this chapter are very basic, I have also paid a lot of attention to their design and styling. For example, what could be more straightforward and cost-effective than a reclaimed wooden pallet? Give it a little more polish by sanding and varnishing, or painting, then team with a futon mattress to create a day-bed or extra seating.

If it's a coffee table you require, how about using four breeze blocks, from builder's merchants, and a large piece of wood or mdf? Paint the surfaces in the colour of your choice, rest the timber on the upturned blocks, and you have a useful industrial-style table that can be assembled when and wherever you need it. Alternatively, try a minimalist occasional table. Divide a long length of bamboo into four equal pieces, then screw one into each corner of a piece of decking, available from DIY stores and garden centres. The mixture of bamboo and ribbed decking achieves a natural yet urban look.

Most people would agree that their home could benefit from a little additional seating.

A recent trend for seating, fabric-covered cubes can be made at home at a fraction of the cost of shop-bought ones. Buy ready-cut foam from an upholstery shop and cover to match your decor.

For a contemporary look, introduce some versatile cube seating. Ready-cut foam cubes can be ordered from upholstery shops, then covered with fabric. I chose a quirky camouflage fabric, but for a more sumptuous feel, use an imitation suede or leather (or the real thing) instead. Whatever you choose, you'll find this cube useful, not only as an extra seat, but as a side table.

Salvage yards are great places to source raw materials – and often the distressed state of the materials adds to the appeal of the finished piece. For instance, an inexpensive railway sleeper, sawn in half, created the basis for a rustic bench that can seat three people comfortably. You could paint the bench, but its unfinished state adds to its character. Soft silk cushions contrast effectively with the rawness of the materials.

Most garden centres now stock large bamboo poles. Cut to length, then screw to a piece of decking to create an occasional table.

A similar idea was developed to create a set of fun floor seats. Each seat was made by gluing a piece of decking onto two sections of red brick edging, which you will find in any garden centre. The seating was intended for a room with a highly patterned carpet and the low seats, partnered with fake sheep skin and scatter cushions, created a Moroccan effect that makes the carpet seem a deliberate part of the scheme.

Once you start to think creatively about everyday materials, your design choices multiply. Whichever effect you want and materials you choose, if you keep the two main principles of comfort and style in mind, you are unlikely to go wrong.

The classic futon-and-pallet arrangement creates extra seating during the day. Use a reclaimed pallet as the base, sanded and varnished or painted.

Moroccan-style floor seats made from paving edging and wooden decking make a patterned carpet appear an intentional part of the scheme. Again, cushions add an element of comfort.

Breeze blocks are light, inexpensive and make ideal legs for a wooden table-top. Stand on end for a coffee table or lay the blocks on their sides and pile one on top of another for a table at dining height.

op-art bench

One key piece of furniture is often all you need to enliven a neutral scheme. If you aim for something that immediately grabs the eye it can help detract from less than exciting surroundings – and this design is undeniably attention-seeking.

The base is a basic flat-packed garden bench – these are surprisingly inexpensive and available from most DIY stores and garden centres. Any slatted bench will do, even one made from metal. A lick of paint conceals the original material, and fake-fur cushions in bright colours add comfort and a quirky touch. The thickness of the fur will conceal any sewing, allowing you to hand-stitch the covers and avoid the complication of a sewing machine. To alter the look, opt for different fabrics and paints: floral fabrics and pastel paints will create a softer effect, while pinstripe and flannel teamed with grey paint or metal will give a harder-edged 'city' feel.

Tactile cushions secured to a slatted garden bench instantly create an exciting and fun perch for two.

how to...

materials and equipment

flat-packed slatted wooden bench

white vinyl silk emulsion paint

6.5cm (2½in) paintbrush

plates in various sizes, for templates

upholstery foam

pencil

scissors

fur fabric in various colours

chalk

white ribbon, 2.5cm (1in) wide, and about 30cm (12in) per cushion

needle and matching threads

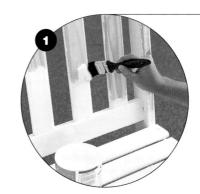

Step 1
Apply an even coat of white emulsion paint over the entire surface of the bench and leave to dry. Brush on a second coat and once again leave to dry.

Step 2
Place a plate face down on the upholstery foam and draw around the outline with a pencil. Cut around the outline with a pair of scissors. Using the different-sized plates as templates cut out as many foam cushions as required.

Step 3
Lay the fabric face down on a flat surface. Place a foam circle on top and chalk around the outline leaving a 5cm (2in) border all round, then cut out. You will need to cut out two fabric circles for every foam cushion.

Step 4

With right-sides facing, place two identical fabric circles together. Hand-stitch around the circles through both thicknesses, leaving a gap of approximately 15cm (6in) in which to insert the foam cushion. Turn the cushion cover the right way out.

Step 5

Take a foam circle that is the same size as the cushion cover and fold it in half. Insert into the cover opening and allow to unfold so that it lies flat inside the cover.

Step 6

Turn in the raw edges along either side of the cover opening and hand-stitch together. Cover all the remaining foam circles in this way.

Step 7

Cut a length of ribbon, approximately 30cm (12in) long, for each cushion. Fold each ribbon in half to find the centre point. Hand stitch the centre point of each ribbon to the centre of each cushion.

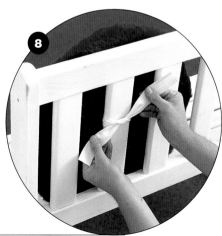

Step 8

Tie the circles securely to the bench.

dining table

When you are on a tight budget or struggling for space, dining furniture can be a problem. Many kitchens are too small to accommodate a dining table and few flats have a designated dining room. This design answers both of these concerns, as not only is it inexpensive to make, but it can be folded away when not in use.

The table started life as a pasting table from a DIY store, which was then covered in a selection of vinyl floor tiles. If the thought of working with tiles is daunting – don't worry, these tiles are very easy to position as they have a self-adhesive backing. All you have to do is cut them to size, peel off the back and stick them down. What's more, as they are meant for the floor they are very hard wearing. When it came to the chairs, I was lucky enough to find these canteen chairs at a local catering equipment company, but you should be able to find something similar at a second-hand store.

A pasting table covered with vinyl floor tiles and matching felt-covered chairs makes for a stylish dining set. Use sophisticated, soft greys and neutral tones, as here, or opt for different colours and fabric to suit your particular scheme.

how to...

materials and equipment

wooden pasting table

white vinyl silk emulsion paint

4cm (1½in) paintbrush

self-adhesive vinyl floor tiles

tape measure

pencil

metal ruler

craft knife

cutting mat or similar

flat-backed
wooden chairs

felt

scissors

spray adhesive

Step 1

Apply an even coat of white emulsion paint to the sides and legs of the table. Leave to dry, and apply a second coat if necessary.

Step 3

Once you are happy with the design, make a note of any tiles that require cutting. Using a tape measure and pencil, mark the cutting line on each of the tiles. To cut out, lay a metal ruler along the cutting line and firmly run a craft knife along its edge.

Step 4

Place all the tiles in position on the table top – do not remove the backing sheet at this point. Starting at one end of the table, peel the backing sheet from the first tile and press in position. Continue working along the table until all the tiles are stuck firmly in place.

Step 2

Leaving the backing paper in place, roughly arrange the tiles on top of the table. Overlap some of the tiles to create different-sized sections and make sure no tiles run over the central hinged area – the tiles must line up along the centre line or else you will not be able to fold the table.

Step 5

Cut strips of felt to roughly the same size as the backs of the chairs. Spray the back of the chairs with glue and press the felt in place, flattening out any bumps or folds as you go. Repeat with the chair seats.

Step 6

To trim the excess fabric and give a neat finish, run a sharp craft knife down the edges of the back and seat of each chair.

cage coffee-table

Uninspired by what was available on the market, I wanted to create a three-dimensional piece that would be functional, yet fun, and a world apart from the standard four legged coffee-table. The finished result looks a lot more complicated to create than it actually is.

The metal cage is a wire basket, which can be found in a variety of sizes at most DIY stores. This was then glued to a painted mdf base. The addition of wheels makes the table more versatile, and the foam balls, from a local toy shop, add yet a further dimension, as the whole piece constantly moves and changes when pushed around the room. I love the modern feel of this piece – the mix of the metal cage, wheels and soft foam balls makes for a coffee-table with a strong contemporary edge, that will look good for many years to come.

This unusual mobile coffee-table consists of a metal basket glued on top of an mdf base. Fill the cage with items of your choice to create a modern-day classic at very little cost.

how to...

materials and equipment

wire basket

mdf, 16mm (½ in) thick

pencil

jigsaw

fine-grade sandpaper

all-purpose silver spray paint

4 castors

screwdriver

screws

foam balls

strong all-purpose glue

Step 1
Place the wire basket face down on the mdf and draw around the outline with a pencil.

Step 3
Working in a well-ventilated room, spray the top and the sides of the mdf base with silver spray paint. Apply the paint in thin coats so that you build up the colour gradually – this will prevent the paint from running or dripping.

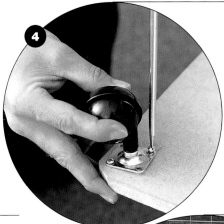

Step 4
Place the mdf face down on a flat surface and position a castor at each of the four corners. Using a screwdriver and screws no longer than the depth of the mdf, screw each castor firmly in position.

Step 2
Cut around the outline with a jigsaw, then sand all the sawn edges smooth.

Step 5
Turn the mdf base over so that it rest on its wheels and place the foam balls on top. Make sure that none of the balls are too close to the edges.

Step 6
Run a line of glue around the edges of the mdf base. Place the wire basket face down on top of the base so that the edges line up with the edges of the mdf base, trapping the balls inside. Hold firmly in place until the glue has hardened.

lighting

the lowdown on lighting

Lighting should add excitement to a room as well as perform a function. In order to do this successfully, you will need to combine different types of lighting to achieve the effects and moods you want.

All homes have some type of common or background lighting. This is usually in the form of a central overhead light fitting. As this creates an all-over light, which casts very few shadows, it does not produce any sort of atmosphere. Although every home needs this basic light source, you will need to take lighting a step further and introduce other forms in order to achieve interesting effects.

First of all decide on what you wish to achieve with your lighting. Ask yourself what you use the room for. Is it a room in which you sit and relax? Is it a working environment, or somewhere to eat or sleep? Look at the background lighting you already have and make a note of its limitations –

what is it failing to do and how could this be rectified by the use of additional lighting? If you are worried that your existing lighting is too dominant, try reducing the wattage of the bulbs or consider fitting dimmer switches so that you can control the level of light.

If you are keen to highlight a favourite object in a room or make the most of a focal point then you need to add directional light, such as an adjustable spotlight, that throws out a small, specific beam. However, if the room is for relaxing, then table lamps that produce a soft, warm glow would be more appropriate. In work spaces the light needs to fall in a large, clear pool over your designated area.

Use old tin cans to make attractive and inexpensive outdoor lights. Remove the labels and wash thoroughly, then pierce a number of times with a nail. Insert tea lights to create atmospheric outdoor lighting.

Don't think your lighting must be wholly practical, however: for sheer atmosphere and fun use decorative lighting, whose purpose is, above all, to be seen. Decorative lighting becomes a focal point in its own right, with efficient illumination secondary to the over-all effect. Some of the ideas in this chapter have been designed with decoration at the forefront. However, for the simplest decorative lighting, candles still can't be beaten for producing movement and atmosphere in a room.

creative lighting

In this chapter I have tried to create pieces that will add drama and originality to your home. Whether you are making-over an existing lamp or creating something new from raw materials, the aim is to make a statement and add interest to the room scheme. As always, I have considered design along with function.

The simplest and most inexpensive forms of lampshade are paper lanterns, which provide the ideal blank canvas for you to personalize. I created three very different looks by sticking a variety of items to a basic shade – paper butterflies for a romantic feel, bright plastic garlands for a touch of kitsch, and white feathers for a floaty, dreamy effect.

A string of lights neatly arranged in a glass vase makes a striking feature. Look out for lights that have large coloured shades for added impact and use to brighten up a dull corner.

One of the most straightforward pieces in this chapter, and I think one of the most effective, has been created by filling a glass vase to the brim with a string of colourful, decorative lights. The result is fun and very contemporary. I've used bauble lights to add depth. Look out for this type of lighting around Christmas time, when it is more readily available, then leave on display throughout the year.

When looking at lighting it is easy to forget about the garden, but it is just as effective outdoors as in. I used old fruit cans as the basis for garden candle holders. I removed the labels then pierced the surfaces several times with a nail. Once lit tea lights are placed inside, tiny shafts of light radiate from within. Thread the cans onto a piece of wire and hang in the garden to lighten up summer barbecues. The same idea can also be applied to small paper bags, placed in single file on a window ledge or along the garden path. For both of these ideas, and any others that involve candlelight, remember to keep an eye on the flames at all times.

Inexpensive paper shades can be given a personal touch by adorning the outside with smaller items such as flowers or feathers.

block taper-holder

A room is not dressed if it doesn't have candles – they create instant atmosphere and can change the look of a room dramatically. The choice of candle holders available today is huge, but as they can be expensive I've devised this easy solution that will look good in all styles of interior.

A brick may seem a bizarre choice for a candle holder but the decorative paint finish has a transforming effect. You can use an ordinary brick to hold household candles, but the small holes in air-vent bricks are perfect for displaying stylish taper candles. The brick was painted with emulsion to give a smooth finish – create more texture by adding a couple of teaspoons of sand to the paint before applying. To prevent the candle holder from scratching your surface, glue felt to the base. You can buy felt circles or 'feet' from department stores or cut your own.

A simple paint effect turns an ordinary air-vent brick into a stylish candle holder. Use to create an effective and inexpensive table centrepiece.

how to...

materials and equipment

air-vent brick

scrap- or newspaper

sample pots of emulsion paint in white or cream, black and stone

4cm (1½in) paint brush

felt circles

strong all-purpose glue

tapers

Step 1

Place the brick face up on scrap paper. Paint the surface with a thick, even coat of white or cream emulsion paint and leave to dry.

Step 2

Dip the bristles of your brush in the black emulsion paint and gently dab over the surface of the brick to create a mottled effect. Leave to dry.

Step 3

Dab the remaining stone-coloured paint over the surface of the brick, as before. This will help soften the overall paint effect. Leave to dry.

Step 4
Turn the brick over and glue a felt circle to each corner (this will prevent the candle holder from scratching the surface it sits on).

Step 5
Slot tapers into the holes. The holder looks particularly effective when only a small number of tapers is used, but the final choice is yours.

industrial-
style lamp

This is a great idea for revitalizing a plain lamp, something which many of us have in our homes. The treatment would also work on paler patterned shades and a variety of bases. What is most appealing about this transformation is not just its simplicity, but how drastic the change is, instantly turning a dated shade and base into a funky lamp.

After gluing washers all over the shade I could have simply sprayed the lamp with silver paint to create a metallic-looking lamp that, in itself, would have been very effective. However, the look was taken one step further by cutting away areas of the shade. Not only does this add more interest to the finished lamp, but it means pin-points of light are thrown out from different areas of the shade to create a striking lighting effect.

For those of you who are not keen on silver, try spraying the lamp with one of the many other metallic spray paints now available, such as copper, bronze or pewter.

Washers add pattern and texture to a plain shade, while cut-out sections allow beams of light to pour out. The metallic finish works well when teamed with natural materials such as wood and stone.

how to...

materials and equipment

plain lamp base and shade

washers

strong all-purpose glue

craft knife

all-purpose silver spray paint

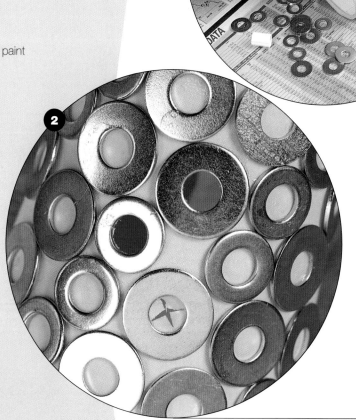

Step 2
To remove the shade at the centres of the washers, pierce the middle with a craft knife and cut away the centre. The more holes you cut the more light will escape from the shade.

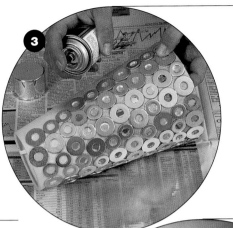

Step 3

Working in a well-ventilated, spray the shade with silver paint, building up the colour in thin, even coats. Leave to dry.

Step 1

Remove the lampshade and set aside the base. Starting at the top of the shade and working down, glue washers over the entire surface of the shade. Leave the glue to dry.

Step 4

Holding the lamp base by its light fixing, spray the surface with silver paint, as before. Leave to dry before attaching the lampshade.

A simpler but equally effective treatment is made by attaching the washers to the edge of the shade, creating a decorative metallic edging.

chicken-wire globe

The basic and inexpensive materials used in this design make the end product even more spectacular. Most of them – the gravel, pot and chicken wire – can be bought at any local DIY store or garden centre, and most of us have a string of lights tucked away somewhere ready for Christmas.

One of the advantages of this piece is its versatility. Mould the chicken wire into the design of your choice to create a lamp that is unique to you and your home.

So be experimental, think about your own room scheme and select a design that complements it. The only thing to remember is to keep the shape fairly simple. I've used a ball cactus as the basis for my design, as it is easy to mould and, I feel, its simplicity contributes to the success of the design. You may prefer a more complex shape, such as a star or sunflower. Whatever you decide, this light will grab everyone's attention as it twinkles away in the corner of your room.

A ball of chicken wire resting on a painted terracotta pot, and inter-woven with a string of lights, turns a dull, dark corner into a focal point.

how to...

materials and equipment

terracotta pot

cream emulsion paint

4cm (1½in) paint brush

chicken wire

strong scissors

newspaper

gravel

string of Christmas lights

masking tape

all-purpose silver spray paint

fine wire

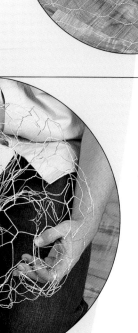

Step 1
Apply one or two coats of emulsion paint to the outside of the terracotta pot, allowing each coat to dry between applications.

Step 2
Cut a large square from the chicken wire – the size you choose will determine the size of the finished lamp. This piece is approximately 50cm (20in) square.

Step 3
Shape the chicken wire into a ball by gently folding in all four corners and moulding the wire in the palm of your hands. Take care when handling the wire as the cut edges of the wire are quite sharp.

Step 4
Scrunch up sheets of newspaper and use to fill the terracotta pot – stopping slightly short of the rim.

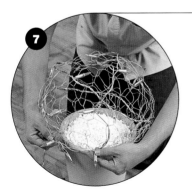

Step 5
Sit the wire in the top of the pot so that it rests on the newspaper. To secure the ball, fill the remainder of the pot with gravel, making sure that it covers the base of the ball completely.

Step 6
Use masking tape to cover each bulb on the string of lights. Working in a well-ventilated area, spray the flex and bulb fittings silver. Once dry, remove the masking tape.

Step 7
Wrap the lights around the wire ball, arranging them so that the bulbs are evenly spaced over the surface.

Step 8
Cut small lengths of thin wire and secure individual lights by looping through the wire ball and twisting tightly around the base of each light. Trim any ends to neaten.

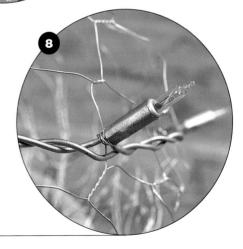

resources

The aim of this book is to provide quick, inexpensive decorating ideas using easily sourced materials. For this reason, most of the materials used in this book can be found in local branches of DIY stores. For bargains, I have also suggested looking in second-hand shops, car boot sales and markets. Below are the major stockists of the materials and equipment used in this book.

B&Q Supercentre
Check your local telephone directory for listings.
Paint, paintbrushes, tools, building equipment, pack-flat furniture

Bulmer's
106 Rea Street
Birmingham B5 6HB
tel: 0121 622 4266
Fake grass

Fancy Silk Store
123 Edgbaston Street
Birmingham
tel: 0121 643 7536
Fabrics

Habitat
Check your local telephone directory for listings.
Furniture and home accessories

Homebase
For details of a branch in your area, call 0645 801800.
Paint, paintbrushes, tools, building equipment, pack-flat furniture

Ikea
Check your local telephone directory for listings.
Furniture and home accessories

Jewson
Check your local telephone directory for listings.
Building materials

John Lewis
Oxford Street
London W1A 1EX
Fabrics and haberdashery

index

index of materials used
illustrations *italic*, methods **bold**

Author's Acknowledgments

This book would not have been possible without
the help and support of the following people, so a
huge thanks goes to Chris and Liam for allowing me
to turn their house into a studio; Nick Smith for letting
us photograph his house; and The Custard Factory
for being such an ideal location. Thanks also to Jo,
Austin and Christian at People, for providing such cool
accessories; Mum and Dad for believing in everything;
and of course, everyone at David & Charles.